Elpida has over 20 years of experience as a teacher and a manager in education. She started teaching at university during her postgraduate studies in Canterbury before moving on to further education and then teaching in a secondary school. She moved to Cambridge to work at a leading independent school where she is now Assistant Principal with a remit for teaching and learning. Drawing on these rich experiences along with degrees in education and special educational needs, including assessing students for learning difficulties, Elpida has compiled this book to help educators maximise their students' potential. She lives in Cambridge with her husband Joel and their cat Kozzie.

Dear Stephen

We are very fortunate that Joe has joined our team-time

I think there's ... but I hope that you read ... of the ...

and ... I don't ... that I can reach you and ... and I will ... this book

Warm wishes

Elpida

For all the teachers who care and are constantly trying to improve.

Dr Elpida S. Christianaki

THE LITTLE BLUE BOOK FOR TEACHERS

58 WAYS TO ENGAGE STUDENTS

AUSTIN MACAULEY PUBLISHERS™

LONDON • CAMBRIDGE • NEW YORK • SHARJAH

A CIP catalogue record for this title is available from the British Library.

ISBN 9781398463202 (Paperback)
ISBN 9781398463219 (ePub e-book)

www.austinmacauley.com

First Published 2022
Austin Macauley Publishers Ltd®
1 Canada Square
Canary Wharf
London
E14 5AA

Table of Contents

'Education is the kindling of a flame.'

– Socrates

Preface

For over 20 years as a teacher and a manager in education, I have found myself creating, learning, cataloguing and then passing on a range of strategies and techniques to improve both my own and my colleagues' teaching and learning.

This catalogue is borne out of practical experience and the privilege of working and sharing ideas with students and teachers across a wide range of ages, from primary school to university, all abilities and both the state and independent sector. Very little has come from studying education, although it has not been for a lack of trying. My bookshelves are groaning with books about teaching. I have dragged myself through four different teaching degrees and undergone more CPD than I care to remember. All these experiences had value and made me a better teacher and manager. Yet still, every year, I find myself going back to the same catalogue of strategies and techniques that I had developed over the years.

This book is just that catalogue. The core idea is that a teacher can read any section quickly and get a good idea for improving delivery. Points are not laboured with an overuse of examples, icons or case studies to divert the reader from the key points.

The best techniques are the ones that are easily applicable and transferable from one subject to the next and in this book, you will find all strategies fit this remit. It is designed to be small enough to fit in your pocket or, more likely, in your bag wedged between folders, marking and your lunchbox! I hope you enjoy it and find yourself returning to it time and again when you need a little bit of inspiration.

Introduction

The focus of this book is on making students eager to participate and enthusiastic about both the learning content and the delivery no matter the topic, subject and current proficiency level of the student.

Part 1 provides different methods for checking students' understanding of previous material while making learners feel secure and confident. It then moves on to demonstrate methods for presenting the next topic in collaboration with the students and details ways to excite students' curiosity about the next aspect of learning.

Part 2 delves deeper into preparing students to process new material while exercising critical thinking without making the delivery dry or difficult but retaining collaboration and enthusiasm. It then moves on to focus on building students' resilience by exposing them to progressively trickier and more unusual questions. Students become more confident of their abilities as learners and are better prepared to 'work things out' for themselves.

Part 1:
Check and Introduce

Section A:
Checking Previous Learning

1. Feigning Ignorance

The teacher can feign ignorance about the previous lesson and ask students questions. These can be:

a. What was covered?
b. What were the key points learned?

The questions can be initially general and then progressively become more specific and more difficult.

2. Matching Activity

The teacher provides students with written questions and answers and asks them to match the correct pairs. The teacher can prepare a handout and ask students to draw a line to connect items from different lists.

Alternatively, the teacher can prepare a PowerPoint and ask students to come to the board and use a board marker to connect points.

Finally, students can be given two sets of envelopes per group and asked to match items from first envelope with items from second envelope on their desk. To increase difficulty, this activity can be timed.

3. Form a Question Chain

The teacher lists the starter questions on the board, slide or handout. The teacher then nominates a student to answer the first question.

This student then nominates a second student to answer any other question.

The second student nominates a third student and so on until all questions have been answered.

4. Mark 'Someone Else's Work'

The teacher creates a fake answer from a pretend student and asks students to work independently, in groups or in pairs to identify the mistakes and apply the relevant mark scheme, if applicable.

5. Pick the Thorn

The teacher asks students to give feedback on how well they think they understand the points covered in a previous lesson.

The teacher can use an online platform and write a key concept and then ask students to select an emoticon to rate the concept.

The teacher can also just ask the students to rate how well they understand a topic by calling out a particular concept and asking them to rate it from 1 to 5 with 1 being the lowest and 5 being the highest level of understanding.

If students are reluctant to tell you what they really think, you can ask them to tear a piece of paper and write down anonymously any concepts they find hard. They can then fold their answer and put it in a box, in a hat or in any other form of container.

6.   Returning Homework

The teacher returns homework and gives all students time to look at the feedback, not just at the grade, and write one point they would like to improve on and how they will do this, e.g., problem with structure so I will plan this essay again. The teacher can go around and make a note of the area for improvement.

This technique allows students to reflect on their own study skills and make suitable amendments. It also boosts resilience.

7.   Quiz

The teacher asks students to answer specific questions under timed conditions. Then ask them to change pen colour and mark their own work.

If the learning is taking place online and the teacher wants the answers to be self-marked, they can create a quick quiz online. There are various free websites which offer this service.

8.   Common Denominator

While marking homework, the teacher makes notes of frequent mistakes. The teacher starts writing examples on the board, then asks the students' help to identify and correct the mistake. They then need to explain their answer.

Once the correct answers have been confirmed, the teacher asks the students to take notes of all the particular examples, highlight the frequent mistakes, add the corrections and then try their hand at similar exercises.

9. Mnemonics

The teacher has previously taught the students a mnemonic to help them remember a long sequence or a complicated process. The teacher waits a few weeks and then at the beginning of the lesson:

a) Writes the mnemonic on the board.
b) Asks students what it stands for.
c) Students need to explain how and where it can be applied.

Warning: Avoid using too many mnemonics and don't use the same annotation for a different concept as you don't want to confuse students.

10. Mini White Boards

Each student has their own whiteboard, eraser and pens. This is easy to make; just laminate a blank piece of A4 paper. The teacher asks students to write quick answers to different questions and then, on the teacher's instruction, hold their whiteboards aloft.

The shorter the answers are for this type of exercise, the better. Consider asking students to write one keyword, definition, note the correct letter from multiple choice questions, solve a short equation or create a quick graph.

11. Mini Student Presentations

At the end of the previous lesson the teacher asked students to prepare a mini presentation showcasing their knowledge of the topics covered.

Examples of such topics can be summarising key points, outlining key rules, presenting different points of view, illustrating detailed graphs and other visuals.

At the beginning of the next lesson, students take turns to deliver their presentations.

Section B: Presenting Lesson Objectives

12. Spot the Similarities

The teacher outlines, in general, the topic of the current lesson. Students are asked to spot any key similarities between what they are about to cover and what they have already seen before. The teacher uses follow-up questions (e.g., why do you think this is the case?) to help students justify their answers.

13. Spot the Differences

Once students have identified similarities across topics, a more challenging exercise will be for students to detect differences. For example, in classics students can identify that both Achilles and Aeneas are epic heroes and both care about military excellence. However, each manifests this quality in distinct ways which informs their characterisation.

14. Put It in Context

The teacher:

a) Presents lesson objectives.
b) Gives a general outline of what will be learnt.

c) Asks students to think of recognisable examples from their everyday life.

15. Make Informed Guesses

a) The teacher orally presents a problem, explains a situation or outlines a setting.
b) Students make informed oral guesses about what will be covered in the lesson.

16. Linking Objectives with Assessment Criteria

The teacher outlines:

a) What will be covered in the lesson (topic – e.g., operation of markets),
b) What students should be able to do by the end of the lesson (e.g. be able to construct a 25-mark answer),
c) The assessment objectives (e.g., knowledge, understanding, analysis and evaluation),
d) The levels of response (e.g., 1 to 5 with 5 being the highest).

Students take note of the above, check the levels of response again and set their own target in reference to what they want to be able to achieve by the end of the current lesson (for example, be able to put together a response that matches minimum level 3). Students share these with their teacher discretely.

17. Work It Out

a) The teacher presents students with a handout that poses a problem (e.g., a puzzle, a case study, an article, etc.).

b) Students must use prior knowledge to answer the question as best as they can.

c) Students share answers with the teacher who helps the learners by prompting them to 'dig deeper' and by providing clues.

d) From the basis of answering the above question, students can make an informed guess about the topic of today's lesson.

18. Tricky Traps

The teacher is aware from experience of a common trap that students fall into when teaching this part of the specification. The teacher alerts students about the trap using specific examples. Students record the main strategies they are keen to use to achieve a solid understanding of the concepts and avoid the traps.

For example, students can come up with a mnemonic or make their own glossary.

19. You Choose!

The teacher presents students with lesson objectives and sets out some different ways of achieving these goals. The teacher asks students to choose their preferred option from the above choices.

Section C: Enthuse and Motivate About Today's Learning

20. Take Me to the End

The teacher shows students the end result of today's lesson. For example, a chemistry experiment that produces an exciting chemical reaction. Students should make informed guesses about how they acquire the knowledge and consider any transferable skills that they can apply to other topics or subjects. Students could consider any other uses in their daily lives.

21. Timeline

The teacher explains the history of an idea. For example, for a scientific subject, the teacher can narrate when the discovery happened, how it came about and how it was originally conceived. The teacher asks students to discuss the value of the idea over time, comparing its importance in the past with the present day and inviting students not only to follow the development of an idea but to identify any present weaknesses and predict its future evolution.

22. Stepping Stones and Flipped Learning

The teacher had previously asked students to complete a worksheet on exponentials which focuses on a specific topic they are due to cover in the present lesson. At the beginning of the lesson, the teacher creates a series of stepping stones that contextualises the students' homework. The teacher then prompts students to bring out their answers which will be used in the middle part of the lesson as a stepping point for completing harder activities and achieving a better understanding. The opportunity for more practice at such an early stage of exposing students to a new concept makes the delivery less teacher-led and more interactive.

23. Tools at the Ready

Teachers should not assume that students have thought about how they are going to organise their notes, files and folders. Give them some options for keeping their learning in order and help them make sense of the information they receive in real time.

It will help students enormously to know how to organise their folder, what sections they should absolutely include, and what notation system makes most sense to them. For example, they could use electronic notes that they share with the teacher, use flashcards to explain to themselves a difficult concept step by step or keep a glossary of tricky concepts which they update during the lesson. The list is endless.

Students will be excited about starting their learning journey, will want to interact more in the lesson and have pride in themselves for personalising and interpreting the topic in a meaningful manner. This will also make it easier for students to revise for their exams.

Part 2: Take It Higher

Section A:
Teaching Thinking Skills

24. Can I Question My Teacher?

The teacher explains to students that questions are welcome. Students understand that anyone can make a mistake and are also encouraged to point out any mistakes the teacher makes. It is fine for the teacher to say, 'Great point, I will look this up and let you know in the next lesson', when students come up with more advanced questions.

25. Signalling

Sometimes it helps students to know when they should just listen and ask questions and when it is time to take notes. Signalling to students will help to clarify expectations, e.g. consider adding an icon as a reminder on a handout such as a question mark or a pencil.

26. Maybe Later?

If students ask questions which are irrelevant to the lesson, the teacher can steer them back to the topic. If students ask complicated and overambitious questions, the teacher can allocate a specific time, where possible, to address these during the lesson. Alternatively, the teacher can ask students to conduct further research and share their findings with the class.

27. Give Me Time

The teacher can allow 40 seconds for students to think of an answer to an oral question. This will make it easier for more students to consider the question and prepare a reply.

28. Working Together

It builds collegiality when the teacher encourages students to try to answer each other's questions before providing an answer. Students' thought processes and efforts are praised, not the students themselves.

29. Tailored Learning

To maximise student participation, the teacher can incorporate easy, medium and harder questions into an exercise. An easy way of doing this without spending too much time creating lots of different handouts is to make one handout where the questions are progressively harder.

For example, a handout can contain ten questions; the first couple of questions will be easy, then we move to harder questions and questions 8–10 are very challenging.

It is a good idea to try out an example working as a whole class together before allocating time for students to work independently.

After working through an example together, give all students the same time and tell them that the expectation is to have tried at least X amount of questions until the time is up.

This liberates students to attempt as many points as they can without feeling too self-conscious.

30. Checking Students' Contributions

The easiest way of knowing if students are actively involved in the session is to keep a tally of contributions. The teacher can make a rudimentary plan of the class to represent students' seating positions in the classroom and then put a tick, a cross or any other note type to keep a tally of students' contributions.

It is only natural for the teacher to lean more towards the student who is happier to provide all the answers and, without even realising it, provide less opportunities to other students to engage with the learning. This strategy is a simple and effective way of checking this tendency.

31. There Is No Back Row

The teacher can use many ways to go through each learner inviting them by name to contribute to the lesson. They can start from one end of the class to the other, they can go backwards first, left-right or the other way, or do it seemingly randomly. They can even ask learners more than once sequentially. The important thing is to keep students on their feet and for all of them to realise that there is no 'back row' in the classroom. Anyone can be asked anything at any given time and that is fine, it is an important part of the learning process.

This technique ensures students engage more in the lesson. It encourages them to pay attention and ask questions so that they are not caught off guard when the teacher asks them to contribute. Therefore, this strategy even breeds more student interaction. A great win!

32. Assign a Timeframe

The teacher is aware of how much time to allocate to each topic during a lesson. As a result, they know when to encourage students to express their points further and share ideas and when briefer answers are required. Sharing this timeframe with the students will help them to become more engaged in the delivery as they understand the sequence and their questions can be more specific to each element.

The students will also know when they have more time to engage the teacher and when they need to pick up the pace.

33. Part of the Whole

It can help students to make sense of new information if they connect it with what they already know. They can do this by drawing mind-maps, making posters, creating spider diagrams or developing any other visual aid which will enable them to understand how the specific relates to the whole.

34. Using Follow-Up Questions to Reinforce Good Learning Habits

The teacher can use follow up questions to help students enhance their answers. For example, a student answering a medium length economics question has remembered to provide a definition for a key term but has not given contextual evidence, referring to the case study.

The teacher can then ask a follow-up question to encourage the student to analyse and evaluate their findings. With each follow-up question, the student is supported further towards a higher-level answer.

35. Checking What They Already Know

Before teaching a new topic, it can be useful to check, either orally or written, what students already know. This makes the learning more student-centred and helps teachers keep track of students' progress.

36. How Often Should We Check Level of Knowledge?

Regular checking of students' understanding helps them hone their skills, practise and develop their reasoning skills.

Students can be asked to take mini tests, do mini performances (for example presentations, debates) or work on harder class questions based on knowledge from previous lessons.

A weekly assessment completed in an environment that simulates as much as possible, final exam setting can boost learners' knowledge and build their resilience. For example, it may not be possible for students to sit a two-hour invigilated assessment on a weekly basis but taking a form of an invigilated assessment in a fraction of the final exam time which emulates in part some of the questions will help the students to build their exam or performance 'endurance'.

37. Comparisons Are Not Always Helpful

We learn best when we feel supported, we are motivated, and we enjoy the learning process. For this to happen, it doesn't help students to feel that they are in constant comparison against their classmates. Students can compare their recent work against their own previous work to track their development, reflect on their revision habits and make amendments.

38. The Goldilocks Paradigm

By tailoring questions for our students so that they are neither too easy nor too hard for them we can make the learning process more rewarding. Posing challenging questions that take students a bit out of their comfort zone without the answer being outside of their reach, will further propel them to succeed.

39. Thinking on Our Feet

The teacher should always be ready to adjust their delivery according to their students' needs.

They can do this by correcting, offering further explanations, allowing the learner to view the same point from a different perspective, giving different examples and providing the leaner with more chances to practise any 'tricky' parts.

If learners have different misconceptions, the teacher can start with correcting what is most essential for the learning process and then move progressively to correct more intricate misconceptions.

40. Going Back to Go Further

When learners get stuck at a certain point, teachers can refrain from providing the answer immediately but instead tell the class that they will assume the role of a student. While the teacher is in the student role, they start by making some basic mistakes which the students should be able to identify. When the teacher hears the correct answer, they come out from the student role and check for understanding.

Once the teacher is happy that the class has a sufficient understanding of this point, they revert to the student role, this time making more nuanced mistakes. This process is repeated until eventually the teacher is adopting the student role regarding the point on which the learners were initially stuck. By taking this conversational approach, the students are able to work together to answer their previous questions and resolve the issue."

41. Break the Code

Teachers can work with their students to create a glossary to explain common 'command' words that appear in exam questions such as 'analyse', 'explain', 'discuss', etc.

Helping learners identify what each command word means will allow them to understand what the examiner is looking for. This will enable them to apply their subject knowledge more effectively to achieve better results.

42. How to Take Homework Higher?

Consider using homework as a basis to engage students in higher order thinking in class.

How is this possible? Say, for example, that learners had to answer different questions on exponentials. You then go through the answers together, identify tricky parts and ask them to do further exercises to help them hone their skills.

No matter what the subject matter is, the teacher can increase the difficulty of the homework question when reattempted in class and use it as a stepping stone to make students more exam-ready.

43. Changing the Style of the Delivery

In order to maintain 'freshness', it helps to visit a colleague, see how they approach their learners, how they involve them in the lesson and get ideas. They can also return the favour as it is easy to get stuck in a rut.

The more the teacher retains enthusiasm about the learning process, the more learners will be keen to engage and contribute to lessons.

44. It Pays to Think About Delivery

It doesn't matter how much time the teacher has invested in creating elaborate resources if they don't know how they want to present these to their learners.

Taking just five minutes to consider the students in each class will improve the lesson considerably and make everyone keener to participate. The teacher should consider students' needs, strengths and weaknesses, and anticipate the best way of delivering the information to them in a way that will engage them.

45. Blind Repetition

Just because a teacher may happen to have parallel classes it doesn't mean that the same delivery will be equally successful in each class. There are many factors to consider such as the levels of knowledge, what time of day they have the lesson, and what these students do before or after the lesson.

46. Show Them That You Care

It helps when the teacher has their students in mind when creating resources. For example, if a teacher knows that a student is reluctant to do grammar exercises but passionate about mountain biking, they can use mountain biking in the exercises.

Offering a topic which engages students, helps them understand its application in real life and offers examples that capture their imagination can make all the difference between a student who is invested in the lesson and one who isn't.

47. The Rest Is Silence!

The teacher can dedicate a good chunk of each lesson to practice and give feedback in an interactive fashion. There should be some time for all learners to rely only on their own skills, ability, knowledge and wits to figure out the solution to an exercise. Teachers present the activity, explain it, offer to do an example together, set a timeframe and then off students go! This means not interrupting students to offer more support, more clarification, to change the question or to make it easier. The rest should be silence!

Section B: Preparing for Exam Performance in a Class Setting

48. Exam Timeframe

Once students learn enough about topic X and can apply assessment criteria, they can practise exam questions on X in class. The teacher can help students allocate specific time for each exam question. They can then try to adhere to the same timeframe they will have in their final exam when answering questions.

49. Tailoring a Bespoke Exam Strategy

Students can consider their needs and perfect their exam strategy. They can decide if they prefer to start from the harder questions in an exam setting or get the easy points first. They can then re-examine the timeframe for each question and make specific decisions about each exam component.

For example, for a 20-mark mini essay question, they may initially allocate five minutes to write the introduction and the conclusion, ten minutes for a main paragraph and five minutes to check their work. After attempting this strategy, they can reflect on whether they should amend it.

50. Practising Longer Exam Questions in Class

In a class setting, students will need to practise all exam components as much as possible but without taking too much time away from the delivery. How can this be achieved when preparing for exam questions that require a considerable amount of time to be answered in full?

For example, students may need to spend 45 minutes to answer a 45-mark question so practising writing the whole answer frequently in class will reduce significantly opportunities for feedback and learning together.

To engage all students and offer variety, the teacher can consider the number of paragraphs in an answer, say four, the topic sentences and then correspond numbers to each topic sentence and allocate these numbers to each student. Next, the teacher can look at all the answers and choose the best example for each paragraph before collating one document and distributing this to the class as good practice.

51. Marking in Class

The teacher can use a brief part of the lesson to mark exercises set in class and offer brief written feedback. During the same time students can be working on a different activity. Once the teacher has finished marking and students have finished their second activity, the teacher can address first any common mistakes from the first exercise and then ask students to provide answers for the second task.

52. Replicating Exam Setting – Real Props

When mimicking exam setting in class, the teacher can progressively incorporate more factors which render the practice even more realistic.

For example, when practising exam questions instead of just adhering to a set timeframe, students can also write on the pre-approved exam board student answer booklet. This will help students acquire a better sense of how much they should write for each question.

53. The Student Expert

Another way of putting the focus on students and helping them to prepare for their final exam is to allocate different topics to each learner and give them time outside the class to prepare a presentation.

This can focus on revising key concepts, going through tricky questions, checking mark schemes, discussing best answers from principal examiners' reports and setting and marking mini exam questions related to their topics. It can extend to role-plays and discussion about props, lessons learnt and sharing practical tips.

54. Conference

Students can be encouraged to attend a conference as a class. This is a unique opportunity to learn from the assessors themselves.

Prior to the event, teachers can give worksheets to students to complete during the conference and encourage them to find out as much information as possible about X, Y, Z by conducting their own independent research. Students can also be prompted to raise questions during the event and participate in answering the speakers' questions.

55. The Student Examiner

Students can be prompted to mark a sample of fake students' work prepared by the teacher. All students can be given the same mark schemes and be asked to mark each element and prepare to justify their answers.

Students then have an examiner standardisation meeting during which time they are supported by the teacher to agree on top, middle and weakest performance from the sample of 'student answers' and adjust grade thresholds accordingly.

This strategy makes the lesson student-centred and allows students to get a better understanding of assessment criteria and grade thresholds.

Section C: Answering Unusual Exam Questions

56. Change Wording of Exam Questions

Students who usually try to learn exam answers by heart end up not answering the exam question in front of them but the one they hoped to have been asked. To help students build their confidence and resilience, the teacher can change the wording of exam questions so that students don't just regurgitate previously learnt content.

57. Increasing the Difficulty

Progressively heightening the level of difficulty of the questions is another way of strengthening students' resilience. For written assessments, the questions can progressively require more abstract thinking, involve harder concepts and can have wordier instructions.

58. 'Those Who Know Do, Those Who Understand Teach'

Teachers can verbalise their thought process when working out answers on the board. This will allow students to have a better understanding of how to reason by emulating a model. In time, students will start thinking of their own way to answer questions.

Teaching thinking skills fosters creativity which, in turn, nurtures students to become active participants of the learning process.